spaces in the light said to be where one/ comes from

Other books by Stephen Ratcliffe

Campion: On Song, Routledge & Kegan Paul, 1981

New York Notes, Tombouctou, 1983

Distance, Avenue B, 1986

Mobile/Mobile, Echo Park Press, 1987

Rustic Diversions, Echo Park Press, 1988

[where late the sweet] BIRDS SANG, O Books, 1989

Sonnets, Potes & Poets, 1989

Before Photography, THE Press, 1991

Metalmorphosis, THE Press, 1991

five, Slim Press, 1991

Sequel to Prose, Zasterle, 1992

spaces in the light said to be where one/ comes from

Stephen Ratcliffe

Potes & Poets Press, Elmwood, Connecticut, 1992

Sections of this poem have appeared in *Avec, Caliban, Cyanosis, Five Fingers Review, furnitures, Nine, O.Ars, Talisman, Temblor, Tyuonyi* and *Writing*. #73 was printed as a broadside by Vita Brevis.

Cover: *Changes and Disappearances, #35* (1979-81) by John Cage, from a series of 35 related engravings with drypoint and photo-etching, courtesy of the Fine Arts Museums of San Francisco, Achenbach Foundation for the Graphic Arts, Crown Point Press Archive, gift of Kathan Brown.

In memorium John Cage

What does it mean to say I "hear" in a different sense
the piano, its sound, the piece, the player, his fluency?
Wittgenstein

1

Every lights on a twig, each butting away the want from leaning
on its tatters, Mediterranean, which clarion
through the house it hangs on
"are you happy?"—among themselves sudden pastel lights
a color known as somnolent beside the dish
the sickle's compass, so much
more than it seems when it gets dark on a page
preparing nothing to do with the ear but more if the color *is*
careless, like water when it makes its nest
on the bank where the white
flash—lines passing
the steps of a circle whose skin would hand
flowering hills—the feeling is of cast down, yet bottles
pinned for days to the ground on a path caught up in the shadow
of home, winter the marrow replies to distance
the watch passing the clock
like sand, the white down in a silence considered
impossible though she breathes air, quiet as the spectrum forgotten
where the crowd was, windows opening
on pulse failing, light
under the filtered fear of shadows of the house where lilies grow
like meaning, nerves, brush.

2

And for all we are a circle of shade, something torn
from the side of a letter, thought the disclosure of distance
witnessed by birds that binds us to the ceiling
too cold always, such shining drives intently haphazard
dust trellises, vine
starts to shoot exacted as cracks
the tumult of its separate in the mid-air wanes
stripped bare for going under the word "trees" the door closes
feeling the wave of a deep you mean to say
Old Master turned in light, wind
who will care?—bits of sunlight like weeds
she reaches for, one finger clipped tentative in the dark
splash on the desert
driving clouds, cars, violets, chance, lifts, tracks
parallel to the clasp of hills and fields, listening no doubt
to reproduce the faint grave evening cast, imagine
twenty feet from the day the others slept
having grown as to no end, the more to draw the stone through the glass
leaves will strew in its descent, or fleeting dusk an animal
dodging bats, whatever she remembers
looking at the wall over a ledge harsher than granite, harmonious
meaning the mirror at the bottom of the page.

3

Sometimes at night, fevers turning the string on the floor
weather wonders which, competent
to tell how memory bound the anatomy visited
by couples in heaven, water in the road not simply a word
but the one division dried
which houses a tremendous blast, another hole for instance, how everything
unfurled at the fire was found cooking supper beforehand
and you in front of the telephone distracted
standing the way to each door, helpless to mail a letter
as if in some continual watch—returns longing to center the name
fêted, thought a terrace bare to the waist with leaves
the morning blows across, the narrow-gashed
foot you hold of scars, the separate fingers of a hand
at length discolored, as when the wound with a sudden music
reason streams brushes against the grate, lifting whomever is calm
to frame you, put your teeth about the rock
which drops swimmers alive as you look, broken of elbows
between minimum veins, so that you alone
among them will remember
how from wall to wall the prologue held, almost invisible, an opening
its atoms willed together, as one sounding half in sleep
a moan the brook treads, strokes trim.

4

Shakes across the thrust, how the ceiling her eyes mount
and scatter there in black, sudden hurting
like something form forgets
to depart, more than hills a pattern
other than yours, the woman being in the window
when all her robes are words and the voice maps, amber studs
in front of the number as the world roars down the radio
the car in the grass defined as if to remember what it said—two stops
together west of these cinders the invisible
saw in sleep the answer
—if asked you may have heard of it, the taste
of gall the mint in someone else's hand
pillowed in trees lifting from the silence closest
to what its color tells you to approve
far from the flow of thought
wherein things sink, as in a picture in your throat
the sensation of precisely what it is not to pass "being in touch"
with always preparing for bed, accurately
and therefore particles of light
the indifferent stands before tangled
in her hair, belt of straw and parallel to its own hollows, sight
deliberate, as if there were no wind against the rock.

5

Do not listen, fuse burning, forget the light slow time of the hour
asleep in the place where the East is desolate, always
damasked, red which makes quiet
too cold for him
profounder by far, tempered with what the palm tosses
as darkness branches innocence under his feet, where drift banks the form
    of life
melted down in a tub—or say your life mirrors the book
reading late, replies
like sleep in the shade appear, find meaning
also touches roses in one
the voice that fills with pleasure
as he thinks of taste, breath, the grass below
to imagine the world thins its pattern—all white, no smell
wise as yours talking in accordance with a tone
you remember but keep not knowing, to what scales prisms space
cannot be split—low-voiced, a gesture which implies
to know the light silences the empty
still familiar pieces of a crowd, each chord turning back awhile in thought
splinters of glass number, stone by stone a sense of passing
the lake surface drowned behind talking
to nothing
of an object instinct cannot reach.

6

Arm under themes and its rasp on the baby, the ceiling says from when
side by side a shape shadows the use of talking, whose swift
various grays close, music
behind the bars something would hear part
of the meaning she herself can free, desire perceptions—every increase
the leafless air failing much as dust through the door remains
nested, the long-drawn breath pictures the transparent
surface behind the door
ready for a change, the storm in the sky
as warning instead of the calm belief clothes in presence, lies
slowly swelling, making sequential the word "paint"
in the background descend while she, slipping out above the way all custom
scales thinking of
leaning on the turn of symmetries, rises the moment her robes are on
—the sky lost in squares, close to smooth when it gets dark
thousands of birds pushed in reverse, consequence
desolate, sliding down the houses branches filled like leaves ending
so visible you lie back rooted, scored, so various feel
ground the picture burns hearing it
by the stove, feeling chances the lens instead of vanishing seems to bear up
under a need to say the last lights, lightening, lens
split at the edge of sound.

7

How sleeping wakes the birds, talk
she hears of words tuned
without words, then witness world in a cloud, dawn
the remembrance of where she thought the spectrum hid, thickness
under the flashlight to the child who spoke as you have
of the enclosure she drives to the east, listens
full of eggs, lemon, wine, a fluent vein
division shakes but moderately, falling not to despair
but deeper than the pavement water enters near her mouth, the words
that must have seen the stone take place the morning
without a mirror, too deep
to remember the house worn as knees, August white
as the old dog who drifts about the gate, tomorrow brushed in front of the wall
leaves shadow as if waking with a start a person names his gauntlet
in the picture of a place with stars falling, surely
the loss driving to work like rain
in nostrils, eyes stoned by a succession of hands, mouth
to call as it invades the green insisting on something, shade and form
and the door into the hall where snow and silk and milk nest
listening to the music talking to yourself
across clearings, mouthing streams
a cloud of tears, a gun.

8

Her voice sometimes at night perched on the heat, an overtone the whorl wove
    to spin a web, fall
with dust through circumstance meaning Eden, roost and nestle, the milk's
mind deferred—tuning confusion
you will pass to the music intensity, a literal
spell the light hangs in the kitchen, equally mapped as arrows, shoes
where she stood opinion fringed, rose thinking over the roof
half-wedged and tossing to catch the musk at the edge of sacrifice, mist
impervious to gravity, always descending to his body the way
water sounds
interrupted by heat, working it down to a stone the stream plays
over, printing branches the sandpaper of vines beyond the silence of quince
jazz, flies, leaves, bottles, brightness falling in air the salt made
feeling grass, the subway upstairs a button under your feet
in the story light shakes across "no" ideally
if she knows the dance, and yet
at night as her desire shifts into the slippered dark feels
the dark his unpremeditated eyes praise, singing still the poem knows
where to find her
light appearing by the margins
the innocence she can't tell stabs the language he dreams in
of repetition among shoes, answers, apple trees, tomorrow and tomorrow
in both senses more even than glass.

9

More salt as a shadow quilts, darkens the wood to be remembered
green in passing, the tongue of a dog whose work is to warm the world
rising in gloves to read the knot wound by its mirror, think
from one room to another conceptions defined
as neighbors—or just the part
easier to count itself a stone breaking, mica-like
according to habit stepping to learn a fraction of why she came
to the one with a light the paper cradled in corners
as if to question were absurd, pleasure the way it sometimes opens
divided by heat, braiding in the sun the arch of a shoe
on a couch so many miles away the car blurs
when called by its right name, the radio words used to arm
sword in hand the noises of things quickly—threshold, say, saxophone
        the moth
said in her eye, her cheek, her lip pierced after the flute's
round of arms wrapped in the quench
of morning sleep, a fire lest the truth indeed flower the furnace
entered at noon the body's heat on its hook at the station
the blast wrecks from within, curved continually
above the surface of a stone picked up
turned this way and that, objects in the open of an almost simple
spinning place the green inspired, one with a roof
or tree or door.

10

Tomorrow worn by such scale, the astonished view
of eyes left, hands seized as the structure
of islands gapes and stares, split-finned and breatheable
but with a difference the waves touch, quickened as if half out of water
a thread crimped with green where he hung it around the edge
of his mouth, the stamp he swallows
whose sting with a sense of how ample the nameable
veins and breadth of an instant flaw would feel, saying one
who calls could think the difficult choice, sometimes come over
his head not knowing the middle of the frame at noon
surprise calls the sinews, tears
him away and would, full of silence and act
glass the house
vines web when looked for in the air above the highway's mouth
whose trees, roots as though flashlight ready and samples full of something
the page fingers now and again between lags, brilliantly
widening the heads of birds to sleep
as if they could fly, eyes closed, hands made of rust
instead of light degrees of color
lost, too late to be swallowed under the floor
absence as the name arrives, exact as the eye he thinks
he thinks faces the wall.

11

Evening, picking repeatedly over rooms in a puzzle of driving
home from the possible, tentative-colored
circles the overpass flares around a dish of milk
last as each plummet quits, as one to be set on a clock
after falling—surely dizzy—smooth as glass
the instant stretches into blanks
she faces on the porch pleasure will prove
edges of light, the walls and roof in a purple dress
she tries to understand listening to the North in the privacy
of its mouth—unconscious in the downstairs window
the curtain she turns to—how
to say shall
check, to think continually
of those who cry "I" am the conversation whose return trees
the shells of panes, a thick choking of sealight
in Paradise equal to another life
of tongues, the wilting
as if to know how many times the faces of home
in the faint hint of plainness her instinct sees rise to put on the colors
white casts as the sun, trimmed
in the street with trees the last syllable
marked, divided as the sidewalk no one she knows remembers.

12

At times the wall parted mouths, someone lowering a voice
home on a board the pillow leaned against
the rain, headed
round the couple walked and slept—a kind of arched bridge
that made position—while the edge of the window
in a corner taking it easy you might say
watching the house as a branch
turns back to start with a rush, smoke
the music cares to melt
as form or reach, which equally shows the book of tobacco tested
in words you lean down the road to drive, drawing near
the balance a circle's shape returns to itself
as if what is given checks the stem
after the gate, thought
like the silence of rooms or a string
soon gone, whose liquid words the number of the house
disturbed by what error, invisible returns the next door back
to your hair with your feet and neck
crossing the weather, no more low-voiced than a gesture
you know moves among the hills it wears down
for a bottle of string the house frayed, milk abandoned
teeth the page dried on the floor.

13

The difference a body begun to spread trees, spins
to break the web destruction thinks
downstairs, felt sometimes a measure of both hands and place
she felt unmapped, the literal brink between lute
and the narrowest of fields, light among rocks the repetition of fine
high grass or the handle she feels forward of the rail
while on her back instead of raised, head
swells, allurement nothing
the color would touch until the house as its own principle
wraps the camera loaded for the blue of air, the oxygen she breathes
on the island behind her a leaf through the smell of water
pointing to the splitting of the wall, the root
should it begin to feather as an instrument motions chant
in measures she can swim
or walk away from, spell in the direction they approach
the finished thumb, phosphorescence travelling as she makes what mouths
in the quilled garden whose emblem, not departure, rivers play
as much of the shadow as she sees
from where the roofs branch over the square
she knows will care a minute in the lamp of her chin
—not much mirror—half salt, neck
of revolver, performance of the family of cells.

14

A litany of sky, place, degree, always keeping
between the blows that register another's touch, demanding
to level the crowd at the wall of an argument
piece by piece in the luck of entrances and exits, parts
a ballad plays in the cannon's sudden mouth, shifts into history measured
falling to where paradise leaves its phrase in the grass
voice by voice, returning to what taste
to show at least its sound
unbodied as arrows she hardly feels until, matched with want
more than the notes shed, the hour subsides in her face thoughtless as it brushes
the wall or sinks—not a word
but shade colors, driving streets in return to question the gray
middle beneath the clock, slowly enough to appear
as light in holes a door multiples
much like praise, no need to say how the picture bellies
round as a knuckle when she licks it, sufficient
to come up with standing alone or pierce
streaks to stay in tune with an arm in light—more
dark at the bottom of the span language "leaves" it is said
distorted in the rendezvous of tongues
the silence he became convinced survives—or the singed voice or eyes
his name forgot sailing from musk that stung like sand, salt.

15

Said like a body both weather and scene
many-colored, a matter of launching stanzas for music
the tree takes to pointing to itself again
round as a field the image receives
or stone on the rim nothing faces, forms turned white to break
what you think at first you know of the wall's look
moving through the city of rooms you visit behind a glass
porch in the abstract—"what happened?" meaning
in front of the house she walks around in, knowing it as a circle of arms
her presence moves from identical shadows to all
said selves, world mistaken
leaving the water only it will change, equal
to looking sees enough—the side of a pressed hand
soundless plural, against which one supposes
more than glass lifts in answer to a voice that hangs
under the blankets on his sister's bed
reading—no, look at the weather
"thing"—his answer tense
in the quilted dark his name was not to open
through the door, position present as something you didn't hear
in the stanzas you think of as divided light, almost talk
of hands hurt, edges on fingers flattening, stunned.

16

Between lights a paper bag, abstract as scales abandoned
the way water enters a glass in wind, accents
as if from the roof were I to walk
toward you in a memoir of the music you whispered I cannot keep
though more and more harmonious the further the flight
turns, lifted from the invisible shape of ashes
you know beyond color, motion, sound
immense and watching still to hear the bright unchangeable sentence
driven from both hands like leaves against pleasure, vacant
as shade and form dressed in a story figures speak
"not so"—a name it will tell you
narrowing the ground at your feet, your face
turned to the wall, swarms of children wheeling to bed
in tones the way the voice as it leaves
the wind just as it is—how talking in the grass
finds the body who matches sounds in her pockets with the words
the mirror faces, "my name"
warm almost without vowels, which seem
until now to feed the air with sleep, picturing what you are
in the story like an arm, music
tilting the hand
a finger no one spoke by word of mouth.

17

A sound to dissolve the turning of
say its tongue to the floor, something around the house voices
a gesture of what seemed to be walls
to make one mute, or like an absence overheard it called
to know that which is useless, stand and wait
at the corner to ask whose eyes
behold a space the circle of color the stone talks of
between walls, therefore in her shade
the film of a city at the point when the phone, shifting attention
until it stops, knows what she wants to remember in the dark
she says she thinks she said—and you, too late
to tell us what we cannot think, the way the word would prove irretrievable
whose margin fades among degrees of something more than thought
pushed off into voices we find under the meaning of shout
and luminous fall, that the "animal"
has driven us to gleams and folds and edges, where sleep
ages since
to leave your eyes waits when she looks beyond somewhere
never travelled, a gesture fingers enclose as when
descending suddenly compels you to open, equals the voice of nobody
quiet, these walls, this hand
propped between my husband on the pillow and my head.

Name and address out of sight
turned up on mouths nobody watched, slowly the oxygen opened like
      thought
in the neon fatigue of questions following you through the street
old words—clear the wires
of what you know from whom, to which under the feeling of light-bound
orange everyone in bodies a house stares back at, hanging out
up the street "what's happening"—to speak of this
like iron in your throat eating harbors, someone a completely
important guest becoming a corner she knows
how you move—already
the objects (random indeed) feeling among others a music like the noise
thought preserved among others who drive at times to a form
more of spaces in the light said to be where one
comes from, without means of changing the person in the door
whose keys, invisible in the new grass, quiet
as if one is the first you lost but fifth when the temperature drops
to become noise—notice the falls of color beyond reach
of one surface solid as the next, the remnants
say "of poetry" for whose sake a hearing that sounds
as if your voice, about to advance
in the white that seems to echo pleasure
should open the gates she notes by morning, light-blown, melts away.

Vanished, so fades which color dissolved in grass
pressed a thing so rooted light melts the music's thought
sense as though cooled at the brim, number
one minute beyond a mouth
in the next heard like a voice riding the air higher than the roof
but how told, more dangerous, the heel swept from a rung
it may be half against, chips "impossibility"
the convulsive declining beat parallel even in the distance
clouds frame, side-throated
piano rousing across the lake merged in the last house
as if to be swallowed in streets it would drop at a touch or drink
maneuvering to absorb the new smell of air, their bodies smoke-pressed
and half-lifted as the light sets, and now the fume of cells
water mirrors, hearing before the stone rushes
no more than essences of leaves—its narrower side keeping
in a basket on the table, like shoes that multiply when her thoughts
compress to what's called
what is going on—"she is near, she is near"—no curtain
to rifle but form and only in the show of legs
on every side exposed, polished
like mazes spreading where the music divides
in a passage once thought private.

With the light she arrives in every day, name
where its breath will be shed
in letters at the window the rain takes off
to answer so, the little bites of a mouth accustomed to running all over
words as to think in the background toward evening, hanging
between flares a pattern of heel and figure ladders
aware in the waste of what houses
return, ankle-deep and stone-carved on a neutral street
half lost in the nearness your arms lean toward, slipping above
the walls and roofs of what are to become now the green-dark diagonals
of indeterminate shape, reversed when close to air-
borne skin, gathered again
as inland as noon on the curve of a road
to what arcs shook, squares called "need" in stone
when it gets dark names on the possibly missing door, who knows
might be settling here?—someone looking to read "leaves"
voices to carry through the house glazed
rhyme, no tone—leaves
shed and still the tongue that all streets will be silent
in your hand the little drops cutting like fibers, distance, the weight
of water that falls over you, space and sleep, fields held
in the color of no color, no dirt, not then.

21

Awkwardly, the spread and lift in standing for a moment outside
a window of sudden feeling
breathing in the air's once anonymous voice
the music he plays to keep you in, so lapping as the mirror scales
the ceiling in a single-light room thought like a body
whitening on the shore of arms that touch
the sun—it is hard to tell
which breath you lie back toward, hang as memory begins
to be written with his own hand against the lawn
the inevitable house of cells
leaves in the air by the gate decked with names, years, a text behind
the eye closing at noon in a dooryard the street
where you stand in the distance
on ground, wind-blown and thunder-dark, the wife and the child
carried as in notes rising and falling but not yet heard
for months—touch come to thresh—spelled
as the motion where comfort is milk and honey made
your echo wrapped in a cloud of accents
building for itself steps that rise from mine to the veil
of sigh-floods, the bracelet measure of all
whose center draws its circle
too late for eyes, lips, hands, hair, or bone.

And whose pendulum crescent, among the daughters in the shadow of
   the house
remembered as veins feeding the milk-fed earth, little or no air
but that silence of voices contracted and deliberate
—picture the ceiling the chair stands under
the invisible thread each shaft of green draws at noon, or white
like an island in the distance behind which nothing is lost
blazes over you, looking—the idea where it was
drops toward the place where walking on the balls of his feet
you sleep, young again and married, the bedroom door
unbolted—where the east was red
your cheek against his arm as he struck, side by side
to the hollow that breaks the silk-formed wall—yet doesn't silence
see how in memory the feeling is of everything leads one
to a point from which the real wife and the hour-
glass waist
moving like the lashes of a doll whose eyes open and close
whose unfolding always believable thoughts mirror the level of water
level the thoughts of air—sure she will initial, cast
as music through the open window of summer
the lake early as evening at her neck, something
making you open your mouth to the fading, thinning throat
preparing the apartment for bed.

23

The whole solo inside what seemed a volcano of yellow margins
without thinking what it was she felt—how I never learned self-discipline
or whose ear touched the fall in circles when he was two
the house in California nothing like the sun
pleasing sound, walks as particles of light the wind blows
above webs fingers back
the broken window, being so defined
things everywhere at hand out of blank, moving thighs
about to walk through the long white room into color driven hollow the drug
would think, shape its head uncertain of the setting
thought plays upon strings the image knows to music, glance, blossom
into somebody's hand she holds the space for
tightly, and he, proud
of her throat in his life when she hears at the door
a woman singing who smiles down upon manhood, misunderstanding
tosses words like echoes at the blue
she could walk, taking her clothes off in the darkness after dinner
drifting hardly faster on the surface than ropes on water
or shadows from a source you say she didn't know
of all things, breast
stretched as she thought what was it she called him
thin for thought, marrow in the bone.

24

Under one commanded to be sound, errors she herself made difficult
years ago, a painting left on a chair in the kitchen
within whose frame elements darker than paint, the pitch fume casts up
ten minutes long, colors in mid-air an hour before the shallows
the breeze spread in its current a glimpse of the heat
a blue car drives through—the more you go
the lighter the man
you thought was no, not drowning, hot sun, cool fire, nurse riding
        forward on a fast train
face to face through the trees with birds at the end of summer, "a line
sounds call the world"
although they do not talk of it, certain enough of ears
in the blue-green-plum-lipped glow of repeat
unplowed-up, others may be found
in the reply his tongue forgot in miles of walls
slanted in a circle from the house at the bottom of the hill
as I said, crowds the lines no angle
but ours can meet
as if to understand, making passes
for a picture you concentrate on the movement of
running in and out of the wind, your fingers across the page
making a room around the bed
iris ripples against the rock.

25

Haphazard, as one would edge his way
when her way goes upon the leafless light, overtakes him
shoot and form, increase means
in the tropics feint of sun, island cloudburst—music also the shape of louvers
cooling vine, a piano on the late show more than the bits of glass
in the door she wanted to enter at the side of the house
diagonal shadows the water passed in walks
—think of the silence that disappears in film exposed to the sun
mirrors drying across the street various grays
resolve, or light in the house
having said nothing of blue, as if there were no space
in the sensation the reader thought
of lamps in trees
a question of art or accident
wound in each thread, the lost-wax of its origin "feeling"
the channel in one sentence, therefore concise
risen out of looking to name its hold
in music "being in touch" like melting, for example
the private air diffused in a pheasant
disappearing, hawk a species
in a similar mood, degree if his mind be sound
that the razor ceases to act.

Staring through light the other at home, left hand break
as if to silver-out the bark, counting
double, tongue of dog
the window motions to eclipse, walls
she could be turning toward downstairs you say
thinking things, stopping
roads because equally as far as step, passing what is part
more than shut closes one room from another, moves
given to the person possibly boarding space
in the middle of her own name, perhaps with nothing
other than "I see a long time"—a cold wind
beyond the approaches objects pass
meaning on a stone, the wall between one's finger's
having thought it part backwards and forwards in the weather of rooms
driven by hands, a residue she knows wastes according to habit
an arm and a leg scaled like air, folded out a fraction
of what was moving in the language of notes
driving sounds, as if it were a thing
one ran or with a light
left a picture of, arms in corners
where everything he does, say, is married
to a question on the radio.

Soon seven, as some have called from sleep pleasure
the way it opens shadows on a wall
grounded, seen
closing more than it divides breathing
over the surface of the room dust touches or the eye pictures
stretching from side to side to the house pulled
through the window, leaves the line
you knew would say mirror
as the car pulls into it, the radio's voice called by its name
in a thought before the words could read, others asking
what sound was to be living in what happened
to notes the music describing shapes
meaning under the tongue
her foot speaks every couple of skies, who knows
whose drive to the rock falls home, how the turn would be spelled
itself more than thread, the world he remembers in such clouds
where in half sleep the cold, against each other's bodies
releasing rust from the side each would part
in turn, many lives
at the station, the code still on its hook
outside the glass door she would have seen close
rock walls, light-gray, leaves overhead.

In contrast to the body the size of a stone, monotonous
in place of lives and objects green as light
she hears the sky spell
in the first place, the shoulder meaning the wind announces
curves for a number the gate fills stone by stone
astonished structures, the turning
when leaves
sang as the scale among regions
after blank or breath, the current's force
as if by instinct nothing but rain—the rest a mouth
beside shapes the angle of days and nights
divided from air the particle speaks, its life wrapped with touches of silver
the difference a pattern in the oxygen admired
through lenses at the end of what
it broke, attached
to what or where the light's curve
with a sense of the passing of privacies, marginal
channels at the edge of the blade you feel
the flaws you think of travelling
between named sound and the difference its hollow fanned
sometimes a bridge to read, sometimes
the page maneuvering the light above the door.

29

Echoes later from the still dry rock, pitch the thumbs
face as the hand rises to watch
in the window, her shoulders perhaps the sound cracked
as milk coming home in a bowl
blankets the face a pair of tongues could point
nodding by the book of curtains—a smell the bed wore
at the foot of the stairs meaning the edge
stiffened, almost cold
one thinks of the street against light
approaching the observer who feels the shock
of "Fire!" "Fire!" which drives the crowd framed by that mirror
down the road, leans forward as he hangs in the dark
pale as swells rocking the child in a tent
one is made aware of, syllables
meaning the house boarded at the end of thought
where what you are will shift in the body you turn over at the door
in all directions, leave straight ahead the dog in a ditch
green fragrance and the paper of sound
whose voice is itself full of a thousand ships, danger
in the ear forms sink when the compass spreads
a circle at each door
turned to the opposite wall, dividing.

30

Called by such a voice, the name his hand shoulders
the second time in a corner without him
now warm and grasping, veins that again hold
the house the music says exists
in a green room padded with silence he wants to tell
someone to pull away from, fingers tangled
in her hair—how committed he is, the innocent wall in front of a bench
like a thought that gathers the water at the roots of trees
or the reason he listens for the car coming back
to forget, still blank
beside the window fingers touch, something of a body
concentrated between where now and again prints and the blue of the sky
when she turns from it, dropping off to sleep as if she knew nothing
but the hand she washed in milk, the world framed in stone
and steel and rust
failing by degrees to think how little steps
through the door—the steps on each side level, already carved
cross-wise by the shadows of guests she heard
one moment the floor at hand, light
breathing against the sudden music his fingers thought
they knew, stones enough for a moment to follow
one by one, down the wide stairs.

31

That moan behind the wall repeating the muscles as water
coming on, as in sleep the wedge invades silver
over and over what candles reflect in the cool of thick, white reach
one walks in bits of sunlight putting together rooms of pieces
next to that road, to imagine both ends
the marks in a mouth and blows over the rest of milk
on the morning of nothing to say, surely stars where we descend
to what little each of us thinks—parallel tracks on the grass another picture
stretched into the blank made of walls and the roof
to think of the next scene, listening
as if the bones were violins, dress paling into the thicket
a bed on one wall painted as if it were speech
clear to such a throat, as stopping
springs from the traffic of fields the air signed in a corner
one looks for in the yard, the glass of ice
a current of questions equal to what is more perhaps
the end of a thing that changes when it gives itself to shares of light
in letters she has seen through, as space turning the pattern
opposite composed seems
the window behind the mirror become a fiction, one blurred
hand drawn in hers, names around the glass
figures suspended as instinct almost to be what will.

So much said, the light hangs in the air an hour since
each street turns by staying, the field heard
on the next page before you read it
divided in front of the house—no one knows quite what to say
of what you remember looking back months at the gate
raining again, hands being turned into the room down the hall
thought beneath a stone the morning changing nothing passed, what then
most kept on the ground the table made in silence
a kind of waiting at some point instead of themselves the sound
of words instinctively used to speak back—no more the line going on to place
branches again like a wall you take in with a rush from the train
alternately, only *deeper than the world* is said to rest
division of the building sounds reform
what we cannot reach not falling—or think some book full of not lines
which lasted but moderately, no simple ranch down the road
but the car you drive in drawing near
the voice in water you drop until it circles
beginning to shape itself, steps into the enclosure of anatomy
as you pass the gate, which closes
like a hand on what you know is air but think
the man in a room who knows to tell
the number of nights hours still, signed error.

33

More to check falling away, what wind writes
as the touch of little more than content
weathers, say that lasting his part divided nothing equally
restless to see one sleeping or eyes at the corner
undoing what you think—a gesture nothing moved to speak of inches
one in the mirror for lack of a piece of string keeps
as a page in the story—how the sun dragged
the nerve to pass when thoughts arm the difference
meaning her face spells in his arms, sometimes through the trees
the play of fingers when they set light down the stairs
sounding an overtone the distance belongs to
to speak of the way one glimpses
senses, forms that is
the last stone heard under the sun beginning
to wait for the flash the syllable recorded among arrows, sons
with the engine running over the grass to feeling
shells instead of his head
raised inside it, inherent in paint as light itself
loaded the camera to forget what you came for, stroke you breathed
beside the words evidence of salt the story of one more stone
on the island moved, dividing
and falling this way down at the door.

The way looks against a post, washes the term
interrupted when the figure in motion stings, the measures
music made of a house he stands in away from light
in different directions as they return, one man
about the middle he has traveled
now that he makes what belongs to him in his boat
work, features in the darkening frame of night whose words double
the notes in his voice printed as silence, tree green
opening the paper of its branches to a house
mirrored where the water sounds
knocking at the door to the square, other hands the leaves work
like taking off a name in the dark of everything
in clothes which spin like the lines
at the mirror's mouth
in books open to the aspirin of memory, sometimes
a brightness in place between the blows
to the one reading signs on the porch, another who listens to the steps
recorded behind them—everyone touching in places
crowded together, wanting a shaft
with holes in the light beside the bed of his book, birds
after all the water made over coming in
thought of in many parts as teeth, eyes, everything.

A little as a calm thing thought
moves among questions, when the taste of say rivers that never touch
voice by voice returning to think which way it will be found
once the sky of near pale light whose narrows
clear thought with music, screen it from what it measures
of sound you are listening so the leaf can stay
—first bent
the eye less hand brushed at the news "speed" echoes the wall
a word shortens in place at last of its edge, ears back
at the corner when the light she hears ascending
in the river color wrapped by the margin
the air in return has breathed
back then to the middle of the wall, answers nothing spoke
which make it not tell—the sides of one leaf
feeling spent in things with stops
air heaving in the door we ask a little ourselves
—how one sees the need to deflect
speech going round and
around the glass whose shank measures under such a breath
the hand itself that held the palm it missed, water
when she licks it, how easily shoulder passes
to shoulder the syllables in the hollow of its ear.

Content, so burnt out that voices too light up
having a glass contract to almost rest in the language
single "leaves enclose," why one sent
down the fold blue
leaves spread out when summer passed the shade and breath lay still
like an instrument figured in the mouth of squares, current
modified in words the weather makes happen—the floor feet forgive
the dog at the bottom of the dark, tongue and sometimes throat
that thirst in the cup of itself is left until broken
before the same as one known *farewell*
in one another's music, hand upon arm fastened to what it knows it is
but at the touch seems to cross from air to ache, scar
in the sand enough to feel what breath
like a body lost to weather or memory in the place where scenes
below rest—rather sense the cracks than waking fall
years after many-colored, broken glass on hands and knees
where not to return your face in thought's branches, which one
by one the magnet points to float the hours between image and shade
sound more a screen from the stone at its head another plays
than sight, birds on the flame before it hung blue
wings if anything changed by number
less soon, buoyed out between walls, cinders.

Station in turn
all white, to break like a hand through the muscle
of someone who threads water in terms of lines, as a mother
lights the figure moving through the bedroom at the foot of the stairs
to something she wrote, every leaf as form appeared to enter what it knows
outside the window, already dividing light from visible light
when she walks in front of the cars
so fast out of nowhere, speechless, a circle of strangers moving from presence
to learning how to hold in the mouth identical
mistakes, imagining in the look a rear-view mirror will change
as you think of her front legs planted, neck stretched, eyes
equal to roots at the grass in the distance leaves shade
starting in small mounds to cross from the right side its progress
directly in front of speed
to an area breathing out of what should I do
—the view is to the window, and between it and the train stops
the way a car beneath the blue scales
toward a stone arched over water, pressed inward, soundlessly
more than the plural of feeling a portion of being various
glass, the tongue between the sound one supposes stands in the evening
growing tired, heard
as an answer holding until the light that holds is gone.

Mica, asleep in this thought of a bed in the next room
and you in the story about to believe what you read is not the truth
of people you drove beside as if it were a freeway, planned
at play in the folds of a quilt whose leaves piled
like sand, like fur—but to tell the shape
first the foot in its still carefully broken light, the house a shadow thins
silences toward an answer as sure in the blanket dark let go
as talking surrounds the car, a look that is
the "circumstance" of something in writing about the garden
in its present position, the letter too loud
thinking for example that by its presence in the world music
has to do with evening distances, how everything untitled dissolves almost
as words remembered in places say at the end of nothing
hanging in a screen, believing that nothing but space and light
between wind on the street and the way you see it
in a prism opened by a knife, abstract
at the edge of inflection
moving without knowing it passed the line as if it were the street
you walk in a circle down the block, something
close to you—air clear
by design in a place wavelengths hide under the music
memory of the form the face lost, most thin.

Let eye look the shape of sound, a cloud she knows that turns
between a climate and the word air would watch
to hear the sign whose presence both
hands forget—which degree
at first vacant, no doubt told the given
form of shade in everything different the story tells
or absent wonders at the light of figures drawn after the pattern
it breathes, silent as the name the second hand writes
"not" to say the reason its vision runs to birds
whose eyes open, flatten quietly the body against the wall
of ground, rosemary and thyme and a feather
planted in the rain or water on a road dressed in white at your feet
—or is she at the door when the lens shapes
light to bed, calls away
tones evening the rocks the voice leaves a line
nothing to ask for but the eyes they find as instruments of each other
a sting and body in the stream water palms, words in a cup
you match with names and faces in the mirror you
reverse, the hand turned after content
who said nothing beside remains here, at last set
as to withstand this light without vowels
being warm, yellow and black and pale red moving to hear.

40

Blue saw in the voice and, suddenly controllable beneath the weight
of leaves thought sparks as it wakes speech, one hand
in the story of birds painted like music
played at the window, minutes close to the day everyone
moving to dissolve whether under its tongue or beside the little it feeds on
in English, bottles to say nothing of salt in a glass, water on the floor
standing in the sound at the base of what he might have been
an instant cast by walls whose height, unknown, bends
to the edge of error—soon too much
with a glimpse of absence like days the very birds called summer
instead of sky the ceiling spent, though useless, asking
"speed to stand and wait," whose eyes above all
light the circle of no color in green
which talks in stone more than shade weaves between walls
hills, a book of matches across the vanishing floor
empty in the other roll of film until it stops at the woman
descending a staircase, phone's location moved in the dark of sleep, who wants
between the pages of the bed to be known, say *what I know* caught
in the light beside the words you wake to
another thing, something more
unequal to the pause I know to breathe, part margin, sphere
one thought of little at first remains.

41

Well beyond rows, the sound of men opposed to moving
across the sky centered by degrees
the body in the act and fragile stands in air, tongues
of others letting you see
the idea cross the shoulder of an episode painted into the ground
their bodies suspended by turns, spinning in thought
to the window of hearing it suck folds again
drawing to one another half-asleep
as rooted, scored—a name
to intersect with eyes and face beyond which silence
closes cannot touch, suddenly beautiful as the photo that lies between child
and dress, name and shadow of a noise the air walls out
all you thought of asking, one by water
appearing to take the place of the words left
from whom to what, to drive as if to a friend's house
up the street from the store reflection touches, orange on Monday
white Tuesday, so cotton after a wash to make
sure as of someone you recognize
the water giving up
becoming before you mean to say it, the object of books meaning air
memory drives to a more spacious blink so hard to guess
one means the quiet is different, breaking.

42

To make of the lost first, getting the form whose movement
a mouth that opens in the dark
surface rises, and secondly to land past falls
inaudible in the wake that sights and remembers cracks
evening beyond reach, to have asked say "here"
as what may within hearing pillow
behind air a breathing the birds sing in answer
to wake, which sounds as if it were one standing still to see
eyes thought of as faces by the river, light-blown and withdrawn, dissolved
the word like a scent rooted in thought a minute past
shadows pressing at the brim of leaves
called the name that found a home near music, how level the air
as wind breaks from a roof the illustration
nothing "impersonal" matters
declining at the sides of distance and light in front of the wheels
sound notes as motion holding in the last house of color
on the street it seems to move until they think without scattering
the next music, sometimes
bend and sometimes gathering in their mirror finished
since hearing streams on the light's edge to find more than leaves the doors shut
slamming space, the other thought as narrower
short, fast—

43

Beginning in the light as heard, wheel on stone
were it ever at the gate between subjects
known as thought, arms and air mounted in the heat
a hand painted to divide into the transparent silence music leaves
two knots finished as one
breath, red mouth, mind you arrive at between your name and the window
the wind shut—how you answer sooner to the words
wanting the picture in the background, beyond it a pattern
of light and the shadow of figures
descending from a sign in the street to walls and diagonal roofs of houses
leading in reverse the plane of air backward, squares thought
sits up, mounds called as before to make red
redder and the floor
curve as if something acted at the end of less
this surface than names in the paper, missing perhaps, door locked
the ground in letters after the air closed
into glass, perhaps not
the first name in the house come to hear it
fall but a reading of stones
under the wheel, what leaf-silence and ear fades to tone
a form breathing in your hand like the visible beat of fragments
branches of the night divide, watching you sleep.

44

Scent if the color is open, the need to know
outside the window hangs a moment filling what in place of air
as presence it seems to remember of a habit, balance
when it is gone how his feet
and pillow tune the music if you play it fast, counting scales
you lift as a mirror bumps the light beyond the ceiling
like bodies in space you turn to motion a shout
you know of people who will ask the shape
until it disappears in the field of written, heard
glass the air leaves as memory
returns to call the ear short of breath and simple
hands pressed together in a crowd passing at the root of lines
another in the door when you turn to the house—and from this outlet streets
voices meant as arms and walls with pictures expanding in the air
the city in a light it measures, holds as thought
as if the landscape talks whose voice spreading in smoke
eyes closed under the spell of mouths, light
burned, alone or sidelong
touch at the compass a face sets in motion
not to say let go, as still at first as the echo of light
until it sets in the count of feet
called "mine."

45

And in the morning the pole beneath a word
seeing double, saying whispers
murder, and some say innocent because of things
we admit we know of eyes, lips and hands at the center of a circle
(more than one bed) the compass makes as it comes
and goes as if between meals
and sex in a land the law knots and meaning
sets free, the child spilled among the shadows of the house
expecting the taste of bone, what the clock
knows of fire and grass
burning, sleep simple, a second dream
with little or no air sucking voices, breasts, names
finished other than mine?—or rather how the body is said
to be born or planned coming back to its chair
feeling my fingers on the map I tell you
I could make, *this* invisible subject
in the distance behind the house
whose head turned down, curve of shoulder
when it drops from the edge of "Yes, this is *it*"
before the vowels, the consonants
[   ] all [nig]ht long [   ]
that something moved leaves in holes and gaps.

[   ] bedroom door, inside a basket
one doesn't want—now turned away the note at his tongue
as he struck the ground, cheek against the hollow
arm that breaks on the sky-blue wall
one doesn't dream, the slow thoughts of an hour
whose eyes open in bed level with water
music heard, water poured into the throat called white
(or rising) shallow at the edges the other girls preparing for bed
in the room they share, recalling from inside the music
in a solo the instrument would never end
(I could read) a photograph spilling
light at the margins, all
we say to stop thinking it wasn't *me*, my voice
a pair of hands on my throat I didn't know the word for
held, sliding beneath the letter the painter's name
tied to the door at night, blue and orange
pictures of the house in California
like the sun, red more than rose
to hear her speak of sound when she walks
against the wind the wind blows, particles of light
webs the sudden beating caught in the air
her fingers loosen, cannot hold.

Hardly the shape of a man, she replies
reading history in the white of the shell that floats
in the shadow on her lap, the head of the other child bruised
marble or bronze, music sentimental in the sense it hides
his blue-veined face the slab his head disturbs
lies on, the door in the air equal
to strings pressing in the piano
waves toss in the illusion rust sticks
in other's mouths, misunderstanding spoken as the silence
she keeps between the water and her clothes, talking a margin
lifting the surface to see her body say in the blue air
thought begins to pour another sound, division
of things possible in books and painting
in a picture the child stood for
balanced in the current
for minutes, its surfaces visible
the way the thickness of heat on water
disappears in a car, the *same* eyes and clothing
you thought he loved (the dead one) tempered with white
riding forward into the lake, trees you thought
at one end a line of stones the book
will take hours to break.

48

All the colors of the spectrum—wine
persimmon, blackberry, honeysuckle, shadows in a few words
the source of sting, tongues, the house whistling
wind the space of sound forgot
to break, miles of hills twice green the slanted motion of air
called finished at the bottom of the window, say
interrupted, the person impatient
an object its wing (wheel) extended into a sphere
facing trees the car drives to the left
of a scene you understand is a picture of speed itself
the moment your fingers acknowledge your neck, its hollows
positioned as you bend across a bed
the color of light, the floor running to the edge
closing your eyes in the drift of shape
—music also—like a cloud, air ajar in the current
you are lost in watching the window suspended in white
the branch filled with pine
morning opening the letter you read in the four o'clock steps
to a door you want to hammer, rub, drag
diagonal against the body holes
open away from, under
or inside an effect similar to stroke.

49

After the line left on the shelf, something melted
say on the tongue like film exposed
a picture of bodies starting to accelerate across the floor
of the still burning house, lights on the wall as if thought were calm
words spoken in place
of bodies with heads, hands, the room full of light
shape gives to air a name for the touch of each thread lost, the manner
of its origin "feeling" in the broadest sense
everything that can be felt, the physical sensation of steam
neither a metaphor nor the channel
of thought between the mirror
and curtain, as if the need to preserve experience
for its own sake follows us across the line
always looking back, the moment never more than content
a set of counters the music parts *knowing*
(as man and woman) "touch"
in itself, the example we forget as clear
tone, *fuses* meaning one's nerves
sense, the passage
in the mind it describes
collected before shaving in the morning, the razor
"goes through me like a spear."

50

When everything in the room, everyone pointing
to the girl's left hand as she walked out
counting from one, double curtains the day in motion
contracted to these walls and this bed, someone's glove set
downstairs rather than listening
stopped, the calling back and forth just as one wanted the same blue
above clouds to be the difference traveled on a thread
from one room to another, "only a small house"
close to the hospital to make her feel
like someone boarding the train, no place for other people
in the appearance of certain "roads" outlined
on foot, shade beyond the wall
exactly as it seems to approach the two parts
left or heard in stone, a nation it wants to sling backwards
using his finger to break the jar
she knows is a part of all things, an inch
apprehending the air folded among stems of plants the moment
like itself acute condemned, notes pretending to change
everything familiar, silence
the fraction of an image as if it were the one thing
left on paper, wide-mouthed, arms folded
say in the other corner first.

One to whom in a sense the report served
drinks each day, five added to seven
on the radio in a car we called rest and sleep, soon left
the ocean the way it numbers currents
here and there, heading to the wall on the hill
when it closes or divides zero by two, the line across the room
tilted in a picture of objects slumped on a sun-lit bed
in the mirror—how many miles you ask
before he doesn't talk, touches the knob he thought
went dead before the words mattered, the *sound* of the words
naming things—colors, notes, claws in hand
the arm on a palate stunned
say tonight, blue if you let it take you across the mouth
speaking of her body (who knows how?) the slow count of smoke
after "coal, coal" the other spells the road to the lake
pitchblack, double-tongued, or arms
wrapped with thread more than faded, half in sleep
as a sound stays, stars, spheres, a number
the moth against the light beginning to go home
without wheels, its other color
her hand on the door as though the air she came through
would hold back, lean forward, or stall.

52

Felt through the surface of two walls, vertical seams, his face slanting
like a stone in the shadow a pencil draws in place of film
in duplicate boxes, eyes and nails
known as air, dust on the paper on his shoulder held
it must have been after rising with hey, ho, the wind and the rain
everywhere enclosed, the door stopped when he appears
at the wall projected as a stone structure
all his own, tiles numbered from the head or hand, a few
ashes after the sun leaves the hill—things worn in the current marked as flowers
descending, a region less pure than ours
peopled with summits, transient suns, sound that swam the Aegean
you have been told to survey the coast, astonished-looking
gapes and bites and stares split, breathable
and sometimes divided below the breast by an actual *pair* of useless fins
its spheres fill with music—fish with wings
small yet clear, a pattern of silver in the corner of a mouth
in the shape of an engine the men declare, what variety the distance
as fast as paint seems to smell, or taste in the eye
of whose stamp we examine when the music swallows itself
around his wrist, a wheel that skips
anchoring its bite in leaves—multiform, woven shades
in the compass a sense of closets, passing green.

53

Green, waist-high, drawn out miles to the edge of folds
of a channel bending south, should you get lost
or feel at home on a map you could spend the night in, little towns
you think of long enough to face
between the name that stands for a window and the road
people are leaving, the way you learn to talk
maneuvering the glass you expect to frame the page above a door
pointed by men whose strokes are beautiful, echo the mirror
water drops on meaning as you wash your face
perhaps at the window between the dresser and wall
when it happens, a suddenly continuous sound of shoulders
on a blanket placed on the floor like a body full of sleep, smell
a point of lavender turned down
the stairs wheels had worn, half-heard in the street
as the note in your hand, the white returning by foot for air
a matter you remember of meaning the wall
stained vermillion, narrow light
aimed at the edge of your feet in the shower, certain bottles moved
to resemble various flat curves modelled toward the top
as fingers the observer would bite
when it pleased him, or play
as thoughts approaching a look that made him ache.

Awkward, tracked, a dog lies down in a street he scarcely knows
can feel the shock of his name, "Fire!" counted
in little places set aside in a house
made of napkins people ignore, the same closed fist
like a line in a chair the child ropes, the compass held by thought
of an island in two syllables lasting to the end of its bone
when the music falls, you who turn over and leave
your smell in a ditch will start in seven directions . . . paper wind
yellow mouth . . . the light itself full of a thousand flakes
spread out on a table, the misshapen center of smoke
watching the compass on the opposite wall
dividing into what is called a symmetry of webs in corners
we have shared—emphatic, identified—then passed
a second time in the silence in my hand—here
the sound says to someone who is calm
standing on a pane of glass as if he believes in nothing
the stem raises to his tongue, somebody who wants to be sealed
in a room of his own making upholstered with light
tangled in her hair, a voice on a bench
at the center of the garage that drives water to the roots
of trees, flowers, rocks, sores the mouth sucks
to forget the thought of its error.

Reason in such a case the flashlight, car coming back through a window
the body entered, music touched between the page
and blue of sky in back of her wrist
perfectly broken, eyes closed as if hearing her talk to herself
framed her hands, breath, lips, hair, belly and heart
of stone or steel and rust—sometimes a picture
on each side of the door he said, standing the story in a little room
beyond the moment it fit—flit—like a thought full-blown
or look the lute whispers perhaps in a closet
with no time to spare, "miss'd"
she said, her eloquence feeling for the last blind stair
in a tone the door shuts behind each syllable
the basket lined with pale blue stones, its hinges worn
by the shade of a key acknowledged to insist on something the foot
cannot move but slides beyond the center of, like a bottle
in the mouth of a woman she will take minutes
to find, her muscles on the cement slipped into clothes
her sister called yellow, bleach, the egg invading conception
cornered to reflect the time that separates what she is
below the wordless surface of speech
half gone in the throat, a fist you hold in your hand
coming down from the circle you imagine it tracks.

56

And in the rest places to stop, hesitate, first the shoulder forward
no matter which way the bone itself appears
to lie on the sheet, or say the next minute is more or less lost
driving together across an ordinary sound
when everything in the sequence sparks, one after the other
a photograph in the newspaper of men suddenly standing
upside down, the places you think about polished smooth, parallel lines
going off the second somebody looks or yields
or falls, given the walls
are white and the roof open in the corner between the downstairs window
and the car, reading and writing sometimes at night
to reproduce the speech of your name
together with what she thought she liked when she looked
at a painting on the wall, perhaps only the cheek
or throat or somebody's wrist stopped
by design in a corner the light gradually touches, branches
allowed to travel toward the noise of birds in the yard
who flew in the air signed "I am"
behind a door, a glass of water on the table
that is a question of sleep or the continual thought
sex returns to others in the name of trees
perhaps distinct, sometimes not.

The rest to be heard in a number of homes without notice
many times the shock of a circle, say in letters
possibly composed of real space in a familiar pattern or form
the house has become five minutes before the person, stretched out
    on the floor at the window
as if in a fiction of events or place where nothing happens
between us, waking, Latin for *decorum*
not to think the air would change to sound or light, birdcalls
meant as the vague habit of feet or the hand one sees holding a hand
toward the east an hour not so much of hair
as color dressed sooner than bed, each door on the street
both odd and even, locks picked, keys found tomorrow on the next page
feeling in the descent of syllables to an unmarked house
you almost passed, divided into space
enough for one to drift in in the shape a person completes
looking at the mirror, her hair cut straight in back
when she leans against the wall a page turns
on the table, the thought of a father who seemed perfectly gentle
when he slept all day or walked the dog to the store
for instance, how the position it takes
opening into a corner like something you instinctively point at
wasn't her mouth, how his head falling out of the sky
can turn the words I might say inside out.

For the same image of twigs at home the pavement of steps
like water, but hot, the place we call the *alternate*
swept back with a brush the light turned
the moment numbers, short or long accents place against a thought
division trees to waste in building the design of a house
whose sound you cannot reach, wind to speak of the company of men
scarcely tasted the next morning
in a car down the road, speed the voice of a bird
you pick up and balance next to your partner, each step a movement
the anatomy of a wheel polished as veins in the spectrum
of clothes or shells on a beach *and so on* washed
then, then the husband loving to wake in a room lights enlarge
to something almost single, an attitude the vocal cords
spell for pleasure or to keep the wind visible
more than content, as weather divided into two parts
gains nothing in reply but a corner of the night she weaves
in a gesture too moved to speak, the dust on the floor
and in the chair more than its bottles, he said
promising to finish a page in the story
she had almost abandoned, all nerve, the air in a glass
that was ice now cold
as well as the fire she knew could again warm.

59

The space a number means or body begun to spread
when she called him like a dog, said he could move his arms to spin a web
to catch the fly in heat, stroke its little legs
or behind the head of what seems to be an overtone sounding of light
spun down the stairs, morning sometimes
like a score the distance measures with an arm
that hardly stretches, limp, tuning to make what the music found
unmapped (in both senses) circumstance one hopes to place
between the adjective and conclusion whose form at the end is a stone
the lute sings when it is done, not to be told in the air
like glass or mile after mile
the movement of a thread drawn to the last syllable
of an answer the shoe found on its side in the grass on the beach
at the end of the road thought to be his hand
played in tune with rocks, bed, blood, a loaf of bread
in the brown-green map of swells
the water inherently paints, objects white or colorless
as the actual substance of a medium one considers loading the camera
between words having to do with blue or green or the principle of a lamp
in another story you forget the purpose of, something
about salt in the body or a half-circle
of names you remember when you smell the map.

Lives (one remembers the page) projecting speed
he begins to wash, splashing the body a second interrupts
with instructions for the throat, ears and eyes
in a house nothing more than to think of an instrument
he can measure when he stands next to the music in a doorway
the curtain motions you to spell as light, the direction
or way you approach a solitary cloud of smoke
she cried, morning listless as a keel
he moves in the sea or a bench nothing will hold
by the frame of its features, another figure in the garden meant
to be read as words with notes the voice watches by heart
a page before silence broke the first of its branches
on the balcony she wants but cannot see, how the road passes
around the square it becomes like taste in the mouth
or the parting of ways she leaves for each of her brothers
like something in a shirt, someone in a mirror
she thinks you will know to speak of fingers before their hand
takes off a coat the moment it leaves the house in a book
everything spins, the line in a watch running north
of a certain bridge in the memory of London
the river proves is a toy, cigarettes
on the stage in place of alcohol, aspirin, white shoes.

61

Vaguely reading, the key in one hand and clothes in the other
pulled as a figure draws a kite, swollen bottles
washed up on the beach one is touching
with people in coats crowded in a circle someone else
wants the door to lock, of all the places demanded in leather and cotton
his book instead catching the man who cuts wood with a hoe
beside the other lake in a story of birds and flowers
as if the cloud were coming forward, *the light* before it is spoken
like exits or entrances in the last scene of a play about a man who saves
    the world
she dreams, coffee in the morning like the road a thought measures
in passing to the next of how many feet
voice by voice returning to the island its water sinks, echoes
the instant ten or a hundred years or more extended
to the place pleasure makes private, near it the blue of air
at daylight the unseen bird whose voice shapes the field it leaves
before what she hears as music feels like sound in the book
were she listening, to learn the faces of the tongue
like a thought brushed through the wall of each word it shortens or sets
as it could to "speed" silence at the white edge of shoulders
above haunches one remembers a moment shook
the throat in a circle of voices the last measure of consent
volumes poured or passed by or ascending.

What passed for color in the name of the hill, a question in the margin
the blanket of air driving as a cloud or birds left
as footprints on the pavement, the air above the street
or desert-white floor of mountains waking to answer the clock
say behind its cover, what she sees when she looks spread as nothing
moves into the last of enough light, the other side of near
like the world a foot can feel when the toe insists
on arms, ears, eyes, shoulders, voices through holes in the water
the body stops in spite of the door when its asks
how clearly is a star heard if I see it (whose glasses) in a picture
such as this, until the hand you missed going to your shirt with its tongue
sufficient in the early autumn light, a pair of long syllables
passing shoulder to shoulder near the hollow of a tree
out of tune (he said) whose notes at first divide into sharps
language closes in its restlessness to be sent back to the air, passed
distorted faces in tents in the snow and the pale blue rider
who takes your hand and brings you back to the hill
north of breath, the rendezvous of word and winter in almost
deserted airports at the mouth of an instrument you agree ran on and on
the afternoon of feeling invaded by what one thinks
one did, or doing in another code the kind
of affection weather makes when it wants to happen.

63

Everyone in a different mouth to whom language gives this excuse
baked with herbs and wine and salt as the second course
in the cup when it grows back to itself, the part
a*well*-known man in another's arms
knowing what it is to be fastened to the wall of a body passing in air
—was it the music at dusk or mosaic of almost too much salt
or the weight of a hand leaning away like a breath
we take together, you asked, the body
memory knows is neither lost in waking nor stranger than the scene
the morning after rain across a line of broken glass
fallen from left to right, someone on the ground on his hands and knees
climbing back to the world feeling declines to take as thought
or the excess of points a magnet stretches like an eye
when ice appears to distract the form of leaves
in spring or heat in the desert, a whispering sound the lip receives
as another wind, longer and more charmed than stone
if anything less durable than the flame
of a blue star can be numberless, birds multiplied to the limit of their voices
a primary instrument instead of lines in arrangements
the music placed between walls
of an accident as opposite to landscape as possible
events in a movement including "ghost."

At times the simplicity of the beat in faces heard, her own music
"the instant . . . it starts" multiplied by the speed of terms
the tree has turned at the edge of white, a margin she knows in the sense
it pauses at one, two, three, four, five at the shift between "man"
and "what" can send her back to think of someone
the first time, the voice stopped (" . . . ") without breaks
moving the continuous figure you read in lines interrupted by the dark
hem of a skirt fast as motion, the stairway at the foot of a room
expressive of content or the visible curve of an answer
dividing what the hand appears to know by what it asks of "beautiful"
the form shapes—wide focus—in conjunction with the body
between a landscape inclusive of what happened
and her shirt in a mouth she remembers
as a pattern of syllables, the needle on a seismograph repeating its lines
in the space called the voice of someone whose presence says
"blades" (this happened) clipped
in a question meaning overlooks, predictable groceries on the shelf
compelling someone else's hand either good enough to eat
or the rearview mirror, the man who looks
at the woman in a car made up
of leaves its mouth watered in the voice of another listener
equal to the moment he senses bounding away.

65

What happens in the distance, lines that leave from the right
looking back at what follows the passage to the window
at the sound of "Psalm," one hand on each pane
pressed the way the body enters water
more than various, like a stone between the palms
one supposes is the blue of a cigarette smell that hangs in a room
like a word you understand but cannot answer, say the hand that lifts
to his shoulder in a story you *pretend* to read about sleep
his eyes closed, the body next to yours in bed
more beautiful than people thought when they wrapped it in a blanket
whose pattern looks like leaves, a pillow in the shape it tells
of his still familiar skin when the light stepped down
a shadowed thing, the sky broken in weather
like silence at the other side of talk
or the name one slips through the door, the envelope
like a friend you write in the garden
"What do you think?"—perhaps the usual thoughts
recorded in volumes of books in the same house a woman erases
by holding her shoulders the way a moment she will remember felt
continuing in the distance on either side of the sea
between two hills it appears to face, how she opens her hand
having placed it in a wind that fills the air.

Diminished, the body moving among its parts at the edge of rhythm
pierced by an inflection of light, knowing
less the sound of limbs
or the space a circle marks in the street
than how many blocks she says she can see, someone
the length of music you notice *is* the form
in the margin, a place active in the sense it isn't skin
that fits the dress or milk the glass it also misses but an element
"separated" into face and head (person or animal)
simultaneously, impressions its meaning cannot help but shape
more in the feel of a name than next-to-last image "I" inspires in contrast
to birds on the wing, "wings"
an arrangement the eye wears in reaction
to itself, calling attention to the white lifted from a cloud
as a particle split into the motion of its cells remains immediate
in a line found in the middle of a page, down or across
"an occasion" to hear or watch the reader
moving toward an end "given" in the idea it approaches
from three directions at once, its momentum no matter what
means "room," a different house for each step
in the pattern between two lines
or works interrupted by the presence of leaves.

How next to measure the example on a couch, sometimes called vacant
or in an alternate scheme *familiar* to the degree it stands alone
as given, the form of age in a building for instance
in the next section of a different dream, one she looks at in Italian
with other experiments selected to continue the seemingly traditional forms
of her subject, particularly at home
where she spins so close to her partner in the dress
she puts on, the smell of different flowers
or story she tells of a figure in the shadow named after Petrarch
called *turn, because* the signal changes directions
to reflect itself in two parts instead of one wide expanse
a second washed away together with her name, to say nothing of music
she repeats or the leaves when they blow somewhere
more than forward, static like words breaking behind words
that open on the table or flatten against a mouth next to numbers
positioned to *create* the web-like structure a body touches
without solution, as if to change the story repeats
an acre of ground in North Carolina, catches her attention
so near the road it never thinks of the man who knocked at the door
dressed when she turned in a snow-white sheet
who fell into the repetoire of arms and hands and lips
repeated instead of shapeless, pillows instead of similar light.

Refrain upstairs, the possible choices
consist of bed, rest and a dark-red fragment arranged
in a scheme the line determines is similar to hills and fields (hard to sing)
evolved from more exotic sources, next to impossible
to the extent that without looking word-for-word at the tone
wrenching a silence that penetrates rocks the original image suggests
its own terms, difference approximate to a brush stroke or change of meaning
the flower connects to its blossom or bird to the count of its notes
a certain allusion to sadness, leaves in the grass
suggesting in size and length of the instrument an anonymous *comment*
the body itself describes at the beginning of a story, two steps forward and
    one back
in a circle corresponding to the sound inherent in "mother"
she repeats, the baby who matches her palms
in the name of its shape on the tongue or upside down in the mirror
(and so on) the hand open more than "reversed" as content
to begin with stones as words—*marble, jet*—read
in a form of sunlight whose vowels build
she says yellow and blue, the seed fifteen minutes in the air
until it hears the surface of the hill approach, suddenly flowers and leaves
moving in a picture whose atmosphere seems to lift
less than the thought of "wind"
itself, an emotion you change in a margin.

Or try to repeat the map without breaks, a continuous perspective
in the series (interrupted) a *set* number of terms
appears to focus, the action following the overall shape a voice
concentrates between people in a story like music you dream in a chair
the minute your hand closes, what really happens at sunset
at the window "no one spoke"
(an expanded version) tilting into the light that somehow rides
above the street crowded with people, everyone painted
moving as if *between* the separation of mouths and phrases in the corner
the title begins with an image of speech in mid-air, pauses
you seem not to hear in the short white space silence
writes to keep it from dragging on the tongue you say is a fragment
of thought, instinct or the sound of tuning the violin
the person being the author isolates
as a form of thinking we "hear" in the current that crawls
out of water, the density of a subject whose impressions function
to push his hands from the table or call in the voice of air
the walls around the house, his hand on the glass
to say nothing deliberate of eyes or ears in "prose" that speaks
as in parables, the other moment part of what is said
over the left shoulder, between the drift
of tongues, a version of the gesture he might have been.

Compare the object in the shape of a voice, elements half-square
suspended a moment in the long shadow of a tone
when it finds the dominant or bends at the upper edge of a wall
out of tune, an error someone is said to have glimpsed
in the absence of pleasure *instead* of sleep, air
called returning to rest in enough light at the ceiling
to stand and wait for the trees to grow or their leaves to look pale
in a corner whose space, though abundant, is useless at the speed of sound
the man replies—imagine the number of bodies scattered
when a stone moves the flowers and grass on a hill, whose eyes
see color in the circle which talks of white
dressed in green—hears "stone" in the shade of his pocket
when he stops a moment between rooms and the phone rings, summarized
as the thought of how a woman in another city seems to appear
to shift location or change her name in a film or play
he remembers—at one point the photo of a child
reading in the kitchen she thinks of between the pages
of a house made of words, at another the end of *what* she says
I know you feel falling asleep, how waking is a thing
the mind moves in the heat of a disaster
someone always thinks is close, its name equal
to earthquake or silence or both.

The climate she is part of when she moves, something more
like the thought of travel than a sphere of voices
equal to the world, notes opposed to sound
sand in the air revives as degrees of meaning the body tastes
when a pressure across the shoulder finds its tongue, the episode of toes
and teeth between lips suspended in the experience of a scene
before he remembered the picture known as *lacrimae*
spinning into the ground, how it was understood to be beautiful
directly west of the light he thought was a window, then hears in his mind
as if the cadence of hair itself were breaking into a color it forgets
to breathe for miles along the various edges of a wall
as you see, the name of the country distinguished by its capital
when the girl with yellow hair looks up
from her room in the tower, a multitude of men on all sides of speech
beyond the gesture her fingers open or close if you wish
—somewhere the flower of course imagines
the body understands when it travels by itself to learn
how the texture of white walls has something to do with the head
touching the pillow it cannot name, how the shoulder suddenly looks
impossible to color once it turns toward the mouth
it asks to shadow, how the book has no idea
the window even wanted to be closed.

Self-conscious, what questions you ask in a thought
the street passing under the trees at night
will add (absurd) watching it disappear, lights on the water in houses
where you walk for close to another hour following the father
whose image is the word October leaves in the grass
by the driveway mentioned in a different play (unvoiced) the first day of school
this year, *what* mother called the feeling of light
reflection touches in prose
perfect the second it fits the space of your skin
a figure turning to the window lights, cars at the intersection
shifting like bodies parked the wrong way on the street behind the house
hours after you ask "what's going on?"—the parable of clothes
when you take them off in the sun or give directions
how to button your father's shirt for lunch
to make ends meet on the table, how you see yourself split
between the button and its hole in the line before color
becomes white—something about stones
you might throw at a bird or fish or the speculations
philosophy makes about the kind of woman who clips her nails
subject to dozens of forms, voices you heard at eleven
set in a landscape someone moved
to clear a space for "the meaning of wind."

What begins as the difference between lines in a book and the person
who writes about objects in "real" (indeed random) situations
in contrast to the second half of the story
where the tones in his name are like distant music
or the memory of such an act—less heard
than impressed as thought itself goes back to a landscape
described as *pastoral*, a form the reader explains as something
more spacious than sublime, as if the light he stood in could be said
to speak without exaggeration of the closure of lips and tongues
when the house is silent, a person in the door one chooses
not to see translated into the voice of the author
"today, tomorrow" the same blood in a flower
lost in the adventure of passion one means to include
as the second movement into darkness, composition in a medium
when the temperature drops or rises to the surface a sparrow plays
before it dives into language, the meaning one finds
the moment the father loses his hand or says what he loves
or asks for the real person to be left on the comfort of a pillow
not in France, breathing again in time to be called *songs*
among leaves a bird consents to wake, its echo
associated in the myth of Day and Night
with the sound of *thrush, blackbird, robin* and *mate*.

A simple thing to prepare the senses, as if it were one voice
in answer to people running up and down the street
or the body clad in white, as if the sun itself were *less* than constant
in its previous or lighter position above the gate she enters
at the end of her throat, a positive step
the negative statement of which gathers in a hollow by the subject
one questions most, not form but the name of a river
or other type of shape "on foot" or "in weather" as one notes
how the speaker *transforms* his choices—or better, what tissue is said
to connect at some point the work of a pencil to one's *vision*
more easily than talk, the look of a dress when someone describes it
in terms you recognize walking into the phrase *your* way, the other person
identified by his tone of voice—unmistakable—like being able to hear
the proverbial needle in a haystack as the parody of himself
compressed into the last line of an experiment
in language, the word for example
passing as one thought of the image of her hand at the window
or description itself as it enters the light, doubles the number of trees
music dissolves when it fades into the green of flowers
(another term) shadows rooted in the world
covered with leaves, a mouth
opening on the air it seems to breathe.

A "foreign" country, a bird in the first bars of music
known in relation to the sound of other senses
if you like—more dangerous than riding in the act of air
or the difference that breaks a tree against the roof, an apparent illustration
of the physical impossibility of getting your hands to drive the car
parallel to the motion of the body in front of you
(pulse of notes, the piano returning to question its complement)
merging into the distance across the lake, how machines are "impersonal"
addressed in a line you can hardly conceive of following the subject
down the block, the way a body levels back and forth
in the passing of an earthquake or rocks in the approach of a river
it is useful to ask the moment the voice stands still, how the occasional fruit
ripens in distance the color of haze, how the woman sees only the edge
of the house on a street which somehow seems to move
more than air—sometimes the sound one hears
as water mirrors the light of leaves or stones broken in a ring
before the infusion of rain, how description is simply a thought
like arms dangling in what you say is another tone of voice
"she" keeps in her head, a basket of shoes or folds in a bathrobe
slamming the door to the room called personification—what is going on
when she gets up from the table or tears
another space in the shadow of leaves in the hall.

To have said the stone at the gate is mine, light that echoes
the wheel of two bodies "near" a bed written
to the person one divides in thought, both hands (quote) transparent
printed as arms and legs embraced in a comparison of letters
addressed to passion, the tone one wants in a mouth
before the window shuts more than what pleases the source
of feeling, the part language plays in the background of a picture
between the pattern of women the painter has chosen
and figures who are particular men in the street, a neutral arrangement
seen as the indeterminate shape of shadows on a wall
whose history is carved in stone
diagonal to the tone of one's reaction to the form of distance
in "paint," how one sleeps more vividly than others
close to skin whose lack of punctuation disappears in the air
in the order of thoughts opening a gate or facing the square of a window
as it used to be, before the practice curve of the road
influenced in a different story by the sequence of what happens
to people who *feel* less than the surface of their names
when it gets dark, no key, the door locked
"so let it go" the woman says, perhaps in words
or letters she washes in a glass
close to someone who misses the phone.

"Leaves" after voices falling in a dream, possibly the animal
under the house or rain that falls "complicated"
by feelings for the image a line breaks
in the conventional sense—"I"/"you"—as a way of seeing
how the music of an object might be played straight up or close to the angle
points in a line attach to the form of "ideas," a shape the ear heard
instead of continuity in a pattern of trees whose legend
fractured by the language of rain on water
exemplifies the "normal" tone of a piano aside from its tone
in the present movement of events, not that music *doesn't* "mean" color
or the branches in leaves a tongue can dress or the little street
at the back of your hand the minute a thought divides
into its visible fragments, the noise of roots released in the ground
the piano held by the color of a body that stops for nothing
if the button is open in place of the way it acts
when it lifts up, standing to say if he wants to change
the meaning or sound of the last line "on earth"
in *musical* form, often printed as the figure who approaches
objects that begin to look "back at you" (page 402) from the window
or glass on a table whose reflections swells
the moment it opens
outside, in place of the person moving air.

The feeling of a habit that seems to acknowledge the body
as it floats in the presence of water, the place itself about to remember
more than waking in the dark to the balance of color and white
his eye tunes to the pillow left on his knee
in scales that mirror the ceiling, how the space of a single room
when the music reaches beyond what you thought was its speed and pitch
turns to the motion of light or symmetry of bodies, wave on wave
of people in the street beginning to touch like a figure
in the key of "Day" the two available shapes of water exhaust
it appears, as if their anatomy could be counted in the language of bones
or leaves under glass or the thread of his own hand
written in a landscape that folds into the father in a narrow bed, asleep
—or has the distance of his voice across the long-drawn note
neglected the inevitable echo of the story
he learned by listening to its closing lines "at the root or foot of a tree"
the eye *drops, his head on the earth* (read stone) *marked*
by what the door appears to hide west of the house
shaped like a procession of cities that stop
on each side of the field he draws into himself, the end passing
the point of a street, yellow and dark-brown leaves
you load into your arms
to the count of the voice part as it rises and pours.

As if something transparent (something transparent) were to hear
you hold the notes in a picture that hangs in the west
expanding distance, the moment you walk in meant to be present
leaves under foot in a line of shadows, the light at the side of your head
measured by the limit of a scene the ear turns to houses in cities
less than objects, how the approach of streets
appears to be the thought of walking on the other side of a hand
close to its companion, whose *feet sooner or later arriving*
ask as in a dream to be carried themselves (in silence) a few notes
whispering in silence that spreads to the recess of leaves
beside the door, the panorama of sound
in the flash of a warning that waits to be broken
when the word comes into our mouths—its light alone flawed
as a substance divorced from its look sets into motion
the terms of plans you see "let go" the tongue
resting in shadows placed at the back
of fruit, flowers or milk less than what proves to follow
in the first note of a cloud that echoes the sympathy
of music, the lamp that breathes "itself" a light
that moves in step counting the morning
"another air," the end told
to see if it will shine in the sun.

What absence meant to double, say as moving in a sphere
the eye misses the hand that draws a circle
the second time in bed (oblique)
instead of the bone itself at the center of the house, what measures
the language of legs and feet whose meaning expects to spill between the play
of parts and the third thought in a gesture full of the taste of milk
in *her* life instead of his, something else about the clock
striking the second morning in a dream finished
when she leaves the house, other voices contracted in names
or rather the air that works to remember the bones of an animal found
at the beginning of the shadow of leaves, the deliberate body
as if tossed back in a picture said to be planned
by the father who sits in a chair you can't hear, *this* map the subject
he spoke of less than *nothing is lost*, the web of summer light
on his hand a metaphor in the "shape" of elements
the meaning of rhythm carves in the shadow behind the impression
of a house, the possibilities of an image again
and again in particular words
the moment one moves to follow adds in response to *why*
take a walk in the light or rest in the distance between two trees
observing the feel of fall colors, the emptiness of stones
in a book whose end is easier to breathe than air.

Starting perhaps in a chair, the scene different in that it looks
a step further into a garden whose color and shape
is said to have surprised the leaf in the next image (or "speaker")
suspended between what happens in the scene before "his life" and a place
—*where, when*—he wants in the sense that a question would swerve
toward the shoulders, the hand as edge of a literal body
the line *suggests* is the sound of talk
"meaning" what it says about the person, a "piano" in whose terms
there is nothing to miss but the subject of light itself
(she has to start somewhere), or say the rhythm is *not* moved
by what is said of leaves in [   ]
brackets understood, the real work of the fragment
confused with the side of her shoulder, the part of desire asleep
in the sound of the bedroom whose door we *hear* unbolted
in a phrase similar to knees, how he turned away
(dash) enough to look as the spark jerks
the first or tenth act that closes the play on a private note
in the key of "Was," an animal from the ground up to his golden tongue
less than the calm of a man who seems to smile when he hears
the side of voices in a cloud or bird in the blue sky
whose bones *complement* the soft, armless
breaks between the reader of the house and its hollow.

The feeling one "drives" to correct, an apparently discernable skid
between the windowsill ("realism") and rain
on a street perceived at a certain "point" as rhythm
in a painting, how its surface propels you to feel the movement
of light in a glass or the thought of a mirror opposite the speaker
whose initials open under water, the chance of legs to be level
in the bed of a story that contradicts itself, the word
for example with eyes at the back of its head
on page 54, the mouth page 25 says
the reader whose tongue unfolds will hear as a statement of "lies"
ironically spoken by the shoulder who refuses sequential logic
meaning to listen below sound, or sometimes write the ear
into a scene the words "paint" by chance as a structure of music
or conversation heard at the bottom of a window (rising) or the lake
        that pours
from the edge of your mouth, sometimes shallow but always green
to the person who occurs after the moment you called
a sudden event, the *form* of language "waiting" for the part
one shares in bed with another who is washing her genitals, pleased
to be hearing her scalp at the end of the second solo
in a room full of people who could read
(as she could) the inside *oh*! of an instrument
the mouth of whose neck might have been glued but wasn't.

How to see what had become too bright, how "unlikely" the room
named in someone else's list of things to forget
in the name of the "wall," to spell
the ear of the painter who believes his passion is more than self-discipline
when he circles back to the blue side of a house in place of talk
in response to the feel of order in Latin, "orange"
because of what the door precipitates when it catches
two or three times a night in the letter used to keep appointments
instead of surprise, the dissolving figures of cells in comparison to music
when it walks or the breath speaks in phrases on the one hand
written as atoms of light, the "ancestor" of an image
on the other a sense of the ground common to a knowledge of allusions
perhaps to the house or children or the perfume on her cheek
the reader "sets in motion" in *that* word, aspirin
for example what is stated when you ask what the wind blows
a "listener" you mean to reply to as soon as "motion"
can be defined, the reason a cycle of noises (tension) happens
at the window whose subject concerns the helpless beating of wings
above "the roof," a body turning to what it hears
at the center of causes a hand drops
in the shape of an image—*Plato's . . . shell*—thinking
of events in a history known as "The World."

Both the play of a thought and sum of its parts, the body
whose "order" is sometimes less than it records
in the sense that one thinks to question the balance of a list
again and again, as the reader might say the title at the edge of space
continues to be "memorable" in the obvious gestures of a room
he doesn't want to know, another illusion described
when nostalgia folds the look of her throat
into a form she keeps in place of air
at the door, the second body the result in part of light
reflected by the quality of emotion in the hand she holds to her head
or the piano whose strings are moved by the woman who *can* say
"I saw" the form of a poem whose speed is monotonous
(*this* "muscle," *these* echoes of "cat") spoken
by the subject in the image of a mouth
called distance, either phrases you expect to be moved by
or the habit of words to "hear" for themselves the reader's perspective
of the "story" rather than something he had wanted to say
about the person in the margin, the surface
possibly of clothes in place of talking she lifts
as if between the balance her body senses and the "moral"
of shadows in sunlight (wet hair)
where she once thought the water had called.

At the outset of still another account the question becomes blue
or white, why the thought of water causes its effects
to be sounded in the bone discussed beyond
possible error, the reason the look she gives herself
in a painting next to the chair is sometimes more than it left
the atmosphere of color she imagined framed the bed, almost the same
visible tear in the surface of the canvas she seemed to touch
the minute before erasing the balance of real shadows in the sense of water
that drives the blue to slip in the next to last picture of the current
you say is the *same* fact, *nearer* the ground but behind it
the way she later thought the air was his
riding to the curve of trees
(anonymous) caught in the sound of the pavement
as it sweeps back down the hill to voices whose talk is of stones
and the weather, the sky that seems to be calling for light
the moment *he* takes the line from the book
you want to repeat for color, hollow enough to spill
a few words at the door as if the ground could speak of what moves
over it, hear the source in rain of small trees
(*but no*) or pleasure of air
that sounds the space of other tongues
returning from the field to clasp and complain.

And so to measure the walls as spots of coral and honey and rose
in a place whose history covers the motion of rocks
reading in a circle of music, the life he remembered the moment
interrupted by folding into the once-closed cover of a bed he calls a fact
of the house, nearly finished, the person who comes to blame
the word for nothing to do but see thought as a window
whose message will end in the name of sleep
(wrong) or the conjunction of people
placed as if to extend the experiment of an evening
parallel to what the eye sees fixed on a pole (sphere) should the wheel
drive the car to the left or color the scene of an angle positive
to the object we understand is next to oblique, the crowd
who passes in and out of speed on the tongue or yellow on water
amounting to the hand that turns a particular page, how the knowledge
    of these words
positioned against or away from the body as it travels miles to the table
of shoulders and breath and teeth or the sound of perspective
in the picture of your face circles back to the color of notes on the page
one is reading, the light of the person recalled
closing the window or watching where the dog "smells" the direction
of paint at the edge of an island less than form
before bed, the slant of air as it filters
into the last leafless part of the curve of speech.

87

The shape also of music as a lattice, its capacity to suspend
the architecture of a maze falling into letters
nothing is said to open but the house, what the glass watches
the morning the piano is wheeled to rest by the window
nostalgia returns to the current of a street
someone enters, the little sounds a door reads to itself
diagonal to wind that blows against the same side of the hand
the line colored it appears as light, sometimes carried
by the body that travels in a blanket on the shelf
like film in a mirror when the sun turns loose
its next finger of news, a picture say as it stands on the ground
at the start of what you know is moving behind the tongue whose destination
is abstract, the way words suddenly stamp the drift of pieces
of a tree or smoke or the last exposed bar of music
before the song accelerates to a finish that resolves talk
as if in the street another car is close to moving simply forward
to where the world is spoken in a book whose meaning
the reader *in response to this task*
thought he had found in the act of what is said
more than once, the view of an object
part of its color and light
in places the effect of which (overlapping) "drives."

To expand the image of light, for instance, as perception limits
how the point of balance in the sound of "leaf" or "green"
begins to *suggest* the level of a literal place
beyond the line, knowing the next step is to focus the *form*
of a face in response to the order of its alternatives
(a reference to people) parallel to the stress that includes emotion
in *this* title, the sources of sound in particular bodies
or break of surfaces attributed to the speaker
whose hand appears to be moving to the sides of its subject
in a pattern that "frames" the end of feeling
(next line)
the image of a neck consistently places in the same room
no matter how one looks at the picture, the same world the person
in reaction to what one begins to see is left of the letter
reads as a fact of previous form, one "view"
exposed to the boundaries of light
in a room which is itself the setting of a place
to stop, the other a sensation of thought which "happens"
the minute after an equally possible shape
falling forward, drawn-out
in the sound of the person turning to listen
to what is given space to think.

Potes & Poets Press, Inc.
181 Edgemont Avenue
Elmwood, CT 06110

POTES AND POETS PRESS PUBLICATIONS

Mickal And, Book 7, *Samsara Congeries*
Bruce Andrews, *Excommunicate*
Bruce Andrews, *Executive Summary*
Bruce Andrews, from *Shut Up*
Todd Baron, *dark as a hat*
Dennis Barone, *The World / The Possibility*
Dennis Barone, *Forms / Froms*
Dennis Barone, *The Book of Discoveries*
Lee Bartlett, *Red Scare*
Beau Beausoleil, *in case / this way two things fall*
Martine Bellen, *Places People Dare Not Enter*
Steve Benson, *Reverse Order*
Steve Benson, *Two Works Based on Performance*
Brita Bergland, *form is bidden*
Charles Bernstein, *Amblyopia*
Charles Bernstein, *Conversation with Henry Hills*
Julia Blumenreich, *Parallelism*
Paul Buck, *No Title*
John Byrum, *Cells*
O. Cadiot / C. Bernstein, *Red, Green & Black*
Abigail Child, *A Motive for Mayhem*
A. Clarke / R. Sheppard, eds., *Floating Capital*
Norman Cole, *Metamorphopsia*
Clark Coolidge, *The Symphony*
Cid Corman, *Essay on Poetry*
Cid Corman, *Root Song*
Beverly Dahlen, *A Reading (11-17)*
Tina Darragh, *a(gain)2st the odds*
Tina Darragh, *Exposed Faces*
Alan Davies, *a an av es*
Alan Davies, *Mnemonotechnics*
Alan Davies, *Riot Now*
Jean Day, from *No Springs Trail*
Ray DiPalma, *The Jukebox of Memnon*
Ray DiPalma, *New Poems*
Ray DiPalma, *14 Poems from Metropolitan Corridor*
Rachel Blau DuPlessis, *Drafts #8 and #9*
Rachel Blau DuPlessis, *Drafts 3-14*
Rachel Blau DuPlessis, *Tabula Rosa*
Johanna Drucker, from *Bookscape*
Theodore Enslin, *Case Book*
Theodore Enslin, *Meditations on Varied Grounds*
Theodore Enslin, *September's Bonfire*
Elaine Equi, from *Decoy*
Norman Fischer, from *Success*
Norman Fischer, *The Devices*
Steven Forth, *Calls This*
Kathleen Fraser, *Giotto : Arena*
Peter Ganick, *Met Honest Stanzas*
Peter Ganick, *Rectangular Morning Poem*
Peter Ganick, *Two Space Six*
Susan Gevirtz, *Korean and Milkhouse*
Robert Grenier, *What I Believe*

Jessica Grim, *It/Ohio*
Carla Harryman, *Vice*
Carla Harryman, *The Words*
Susan Howe, *Federalist 10*
Janet Hunter, *in the absence of alphabets*
P. Inman, *backbite*
P. Inman, *Think of One*
P. Inman, *waver*
Andrew Levy, *Reading Places, Reading Times*
Steve MacCaffery, from *Theory of Sediment*
Jackson Mac Low, *Prose & Verse from the Early 80's*
Jackson Mac Low, *Twenties (8-25)*
Barbara Moraff, *Learning to Move*
Laura Moriarty, *the goddess*
Sheila E. Murphy, *Literal Ponds*
Melanie Neilson, *Civil Noir*
Janette Orr, *The Balcony of Escape*
Jena Osman, *Ellerby's Observatory*
Gil Ott, *Public Domain*
Maureen Owen, *Imaginary Income*
Rochelle Owens, from *Luca*
Bob Perelman, *Two Poems*
Larry Price, *Work in Progress*
Keith Rahmings, *Printouts*
Dan Raphael, *The Matter What Is*
Dan Raphael, *Oops Gotta Go*
Dan Raphael, *Zone du Jour*
Stephen Ratcliffe, *Sonnets*
Joan Retallack, *Western Civ Cont'd*
Maria Richard, *Secodary Image / Whisper Omega*
Susan Roberts, *cherries in the afternoon*
Susan Roberts, *dab / a calling in*
Kit Robinson, *The Champagne of Concrete*
Kit Robinson, *Up early*
Leslie Scalapino, *clarinet part I heard*
Leslie Scalapino, *How Phenomena Appear to Unfold*
Laurie Schneider, *Pieces of Two*
Spencer Selby, *Accident Potential*
Spencer Selby, *House of Before*
Gail Sher, *w/*
James Sherry, *Lazy Sonnets*
Ron Silliman, *B A R T*
Ron Silliman, *Lit*
Ron Silliman, from *Paradise*
Pete Spence, *Almanak*
Pete Spence, *Elaborate at the Outline*
Thomas Taylor, *The One, The Same, and The Other, 7-9*
Diane Ward, *Being Another / Locating in the World*
Diane Ward, *Crossing*
Craig Watson, *The Asks*
Barret Watten, from *Two Recent Works*
Hannah Weiner, *Nijole's House*